To Aun ♡ P9-CDI-643
whose love of animals
defines your very being —
This book will make
you cry.
One of my favorites:
Pg. 156

Love,   25 DEC 95
Lulu

*Un*leashed

*Un*leashed

Poems
by Writers'
Dogs

Edited by
Amy Hempel *and*
Jim Shepard

Crown Publishers, Inc.
New York

"My Shepherd" from *Hinge & Sign*, copyright © 1994 by Heather McHugh, Wesleyan University Press, by permission of the University Press of New England.

"How to Like It" from *Cemetery Nights* by Stephen Dobyns, copyright © 1987 by Stephen Dobyns. Used by permission of Viking Penguin, a division of Penguin Books U.S.A. Inc.

"The Dog" from *Leaving Another Kingdom: Selected Poems* by Gerald Stern, copyright © 1990 by Gerald Stern. Used by permission of HarperCollins Publishers.

Fifty percent of the authors' royalties are being donated to the Company of Animals Fund, which distributes contributions to a range of charities that benefit animals. The Company of Animals Funds can be reached at 1623 Clifton Avenue, Columbus, Ohio 43203

Published by Crown Publishers, Inc.,

201 East 50th Street, New York, New York 10022.

Member of the Crown Publishing Group.

Random House, Inc. New York, Toronto, London, Sydney, Auckland

CROWN is a trademark of Crown Publishers, Inc.

Manufactured in the United States of America

Design by Linda Kocur

Library of Congress Cataloging-in-Publication Data

Unleashed: poems by writers' dogs / edited by Amy Hempel and Jim Shepard-1st ed.

1. American poetry-20th century. 2. Dogs-poetry.

I. Hempel, Amy. II. Shepard, Jim.

PS595.D63U55 1995811.008`035-dc2094-47946 CIP

ISBN 0-517-70140-5

10 9 8 7 6 5 4 3 2 1

First Edition

In memory of Stephen M. Kritsick, D.V.M.

Contents

Canine Nervosa

Substance Abuse

Rescue

Theology

Memento Mori

Introduction

his project began, as so many literary ventures do, on a drunken New Year's fishing trip down in the Florida Keys. Bob Shacochis, Mark Richard, and Bob's dog, Frank, were ringing in the New Year around a campfire when Frank, an Irish Setter, was moved to verse. The poem, according to Bob, was titled "Wind," and follows in its entirety:

Leaves—I thought they were birds.

This was followed, according to Mark, by an ambitious sequel, "Wind II":

Tangled cassette tapes
behind Tower Records,
I thought it was rats—
it was *rats!*

Mark recited the poems to Amy, who transcribed them and sent them on to William Wegman, who responded with this drawing:

Amy told Jim and Jim sent back two poems that his dog, Audrey, immediately composed; he said that Audrey still had that sonnet cycle, but she wasn't letting *that* go until the metrics were exactly right.

Amy's dog, Audie, weighed in with the lament for a lost love that appears later in the anthology. The poems began circulating among our writer friends, all of whom answered with their own dog's poems.

Then, with the half-formed notion of collecting them into a book, we began to actively solicit poems.

Denis Johnson sent in his Great Dane Harold's poem about his favorite place, a dream restaurant called "Harold's Bowl and Food." "This was once a very long piece," Denis wrote. "Many who read it felt it rivaled the great epics, kind of a bow-wow *Beowulf.*"

Rick Bass first begged to send money or blood instead of poetry. Yet, eventually, his dog Homer produced—what else?—"The Odyssey," with this postscript from Rick: "I wouldn't have thought a wild horse team could drag me into fooling with poetry. I miss the confidence of 'real' sentences. I shan't go near it again."

Lynda Barry's late poodle, Bob Barker, may be best known as the model for Lynda's cartoon, "Poodle With a Mohawk." For us, she re-creates Bob Barker's bad acid trip in the seventies. Lynda said she hadn't written poetry since junior high, and found that her style "hadn't changed in twenty-five years."

And leave it to the director of the Poetry Society of America, Elise Paschen, to try out an Urdu form called *ghazals*—for a Yorkie!

We discovered a previously published poem that set an early benchmark: Ben Sonnenberg's "Stay," which closes this collection. Later we came upon the poems by Heather McHugh, Gerald Stern, and Stephen Dobyns; all other poems were commissioned for this book.

The most surprising contributor to *Unleashed* may be Natalie Kusz. Her extraordinary memoir, *Road Song*, turns on a hellish event. When she was seven, Natalie was attacked and nearly killed by a pack of dogs in Alaska. Today she lives with a rescued greyhound, Julio. The two poems in Julio's voice featured here speak to the reciprocal nature of rescue.

Several writers with living dogs chose to give voice to their dogs who have died. Maxine Kumin and Kate Clark Spencer contributed beautiful poems in this manner.

There is a tradition of writing in the voice of a dog that begins, as best we can tell, with Alexander Pope in the eighteenth century:

> *I am his Highness' dog at Kew;*
> *Pray Tell me, sir, whose dog are you?*

It continues up through Virginia Woolf's *Flush*, to Leon Rooke's novel, *Shakespeare's Dog*, William Matthews' poem, "Homer's Seeing-Eye Dog," and Thom Gunn's "Yoko." We thought of poems that could have (should have!) been written by dogs whose literary owners were no longer alive: "Back Off!" or "I Sniff Rears But I Draw the Line Here" by J. R. Ackerley's Tulip.

We collected rhymes in search of poems ("Science Diet?/Yeah—*you* try it" by Pearson Marx) and promising starts that didn't go any further (from Mark Richard's "What Do You Mean, 'Bad Dog'?"—"I could have broken a tooth/on his Rolex").

We assume everyone responded, as we had, to the opportunity to have a good laugh at our dogs' expense. Or, to take the high road, the desire to hear the dogs' own voices, as we imagine them.

Which reminded us of one of the principal ways we came to recognize each other as friends: the way we both spoke not only for *our* dogs, but for all dogs.

That impulse is more complicated than simple anthropomorphism, and is different from writing a poem *about* a dog. It is an attempt at translation; it comes from watching a dog and believing we can interpret what we see. It bespeaks another kind of intimacy ("Yes," the cynic says. "Invented").

Not surprisingly, our expectations are overturned: Is the love unconditional? Are dogs nonjudgmental? Does their happiness derive from pleasing their masters? "Masters"?

One thing we were sure of: part of our happiness derived from pleasing *them*—the dogs we know, and, it occurred to us, the dogs we didn't know.

So we decided to give to a range of animal welfare agencies every last cent we make on this book.

Actually, we're devoting only half. But still—half!

Think of it as our benefit for the boneless.

So we're *not* Michael Rosen! What have *you* done for animals lately?

We have done what vocational guidance counselors recommend: find a thing you do anyway, and find a way to make it pay. And for us the surprise was no surprise at all—page after page of love poems.

Belles
Lettres

Jill Ciment

Mommy

You do not do, you do not do
Any more, pig's hoof
On which I have chewed like a rat
For six hours in the dark
Barely daring to breathe or bark.

Mommy, I have had to feed myself
You didn't come home in time
Plastic heavy, a bag full of garbage
Ghastly leftovers with one meatless bone
Ach, woof.

A car, a car
Chugging me off like a dog
A dog to the cleaners, the vet
I begin to talk like a dog
I think I may well be a dog.

Not God but God spelled backwards
So tiny any shoe could squash me
Every puppy loves a dominatrix
The boot on the paw, the brutess
Lick the boot of a brute like you.

Mommy, I bit your pretty red cushion in two
I was hungry when you left at three
At five, I tried to claw through the door
And get back, back, back to you.
I knew garbage bones wouldn't do.

So mommy, I'm finally through
The black answering machine's been chewed off at the wire
The messages can't worm through.

—Sadie

Jim Shepard

Love Song of Audrey

The door, friends, will not
Open. My kidneys urge
The tedious quotidian.
I have measured out my life
With quiet whines.

I grow old . . . I grow old . . .
In endless dogs' manure I'll have rolled.

No! I am not Ch. Dandie Dinsmore,
Nor was meant to be;
Just a beta dog, one that will do
To swell a pack, start a fight or two
Advise the alpha, deferential,
Glad to be of use,
A rear-sniffer, meticulous,
Politic, cautious, a bit obtuse.

Shall I drink from the toilet? Do I dare steal from the plate?
I shall sleep upon their bed, on those nights they return late.
I shall steal away his slipper, then steal away its mate.

—_Audrey_

Lily Tuck

Sniff

I

If you can sniff out danger and keep barking
When those around you seem to doubt the cause
And all they find to do is keep remarking
Don't track up the carpet with your paws!
If you can lick the hand of Him who needs you
and realize it's really no mistake
when that hand that somehow failed to feed you
Feeds itself the whole darn sirloin steak

II

If you can hold your water when about you
Dogs are losing theirs and He is blaming it on you
If you can coolly live with "sit" as well as "git"
And rush to entertain Him when He dons his mitt
If you can wait and not be tired by waiting
while He pursues a poker hand or other Dada
Like watching TV football or pretending to be mating
Testing to the limit your fortune and blada

III

If you keep from whining when Master lets it slip
You're not to be included on the hunting trip
or when Their own behavior civility ignores
And uncomprehendingly They prefer their company to yours
If you can keep your calm, not lose your noodle
At passing Pekes or mincing sweatered Poodles
If stoically you do not show you're stricken
When once again They eye an orphan kitten

IV

If you can uncomplaining spend the day
In solitude and when it ends
Greet those who finally return to play
As long lost friends
And if in digging, without damage to a single rose
You find your long lost bone on which to sup
You'll have acquired a hound's discerning nose
And—what is more—you'll be a dog, my pup!

—Duncan Tuck

William Tester

Complacencies of the Fenced Yard

Huh-huh *huh*-huh *huh*-huh *huh*-huh
Huh-huh *huh*-huh *huh*-huh *huh*-huh
Huh-huh *huh*-huh *huh*-huh *huh*-huh
Huh-huh *rm*-huh *huh*-huh *huh*-huh *huh*
Huh-huh *huh*-huh *huh*-huh *huh*-huh

—*Skipper*

Amy Hempel

Rain

The rain washed his paw
prints from my garden. Ice cream
would help—in a cone?

—*Audie*

Merrill Markoe

Ballad of Winky

Walkin down that long lonesome highway
Left my collar and my tags behind
Walkin down that long lonesome highway, babe
Following that straight yellow line
Girl comes up and grabs me.
Babe, that was the end of the line.

Takes me back to her place.
Carries me through her front door
Traps me in the bathroom
Never saw that highway no more.
Now she calls me "Winky."
And I spend the day licking the floor.

Now I'm walkin down that long lonesome hallway
Headin for the kitchen again
All I want to do is eat everything
Then I want to eat it all again.
I need way more food, Babe.
Four-course meals at 8, 12, 6 and 10.

(reprise chorus)

—*Winky*

Chow

Charles Baxter

Dog Kibble: A Villanelle

Life is never meaningless: there is always food.
All day I sit upon the stairs, nose between the bars,
and consider kibble—its smell, its taste, its _mood_—

and I am happy. We walk back to the woods
after lunch (me and the humans) and under leaves there are
so many dark crunchy things to eat that I should

not eat but I eat anyway. They are so good!
Even when they make me sick at home or in the car,
I like them. I like to eat. I brood

about the taste of kibble hours before it's chewed.
They keep my meals in the kitchen in a plastic jar.
Don't put me on your couch, please, Dr. Freud,

I'm sweet and simple and I'm good.
When I'm sad or sick, not up to par,
I sleep downstairs curled near the toilet. I'm not crude.

I've known shame, and joy, and I have viewed
delicious sights. I don't wander. I don't go far.
Life isn't meaningless because there's food.
Consider kibble: its smell, its taste, its mood.

—Tasha

Karen Shepard

Birch

You gonna eat that?
You gonna eat that?
You gonna eat that?

I'll eat that.

—_Birch_

Ron Carlson

Max Who Caught a Car

When I found out that one of my years was seven of theirs, I started biting absolutely everything.

—Max Carlson

I'm now a legend underneath this porch
where old age has me tethered in the yard,
and every young pup carries his own torch
to me, the dog that caught a '60 Ford.

The story's known from L.A. to New York,
how I dragged the Fairlane back onto the grass
and chewed it up like so much tender pork.
It took me years to swallow all that glass.

And still these young dogs come to see if I
can offer any help with their technique;
they scratch and piss and bark into the sky,
macho doggy stardom what they seek.

I smile at their bravado, all that toil,
and then I sleep, as always, drooling oil.

—Max Carlson, Australian shepherd, b. January 1, 1983

Ron Hansen

Do Not Let Skeezix Go in There:
Winslow's Villanelle

Do not let Skeezix go in there.
Alpo's expensive; food isn't free.
Wise dogs do not like to share.

I'll kill the cat if you don't dare.
I haven't been full since I was three.
Do not let Skeezix go in there.

You got him first but I don't care.
Homes need just one pet, and that's me.
Wise dogs do not like to share.

Lazy? Dull? All he does is stare.
Hairball's his name; his brain is a pea.
Do not let Skeezix go in there.

Won't chase; won't bark; won't play; isn't fair.
Hates rides and walks. Why not let him be?
Wise dogs do not like to share.

The kitchen's mine; I'll lick it bare.
And leftovers? Even they're for me.
Do not let Skeezix go in there.
Winslow does not like to share.

—*Winslow*

Denis Johnson

Harold's Bowl and Food

Bowl bowl bowl bowl bowl
Food food food food food
The miracle of the heavenly restaurant
I this mouth this
great dark sad evening
Suddenly they come for me in a limousine
How could I have believed I was vanquished
I never lay slain I
am the victor this parade is for me
Now they have led me to the doors of God
Long ago and forever
I was in this place
on the other side of eating
where I am full and the empty
bowl is beautiful

       —Harold

John Irving

Untitled

All dogs prefer prose, especially this one; I died in the summer
of 1965, following an episode with unrisen bread—I ate a bowl
of dough and then went to sleep in the sun.

Big mistake.

—Marrow

The Good
Life

Nietzsche Possessed

Dreamcat. Fonk. What? Scurrr. Ah,
canfood. We're awake now: canfood.
Canfood. Good. Lickbowl. Good.
Door. Dooroutnow. Look. I'm looking.
What? Doorwhat? Doorout right? Right?
Knobnow. Good. I'm gone. Cat.
Realcat now. Hot damn. Damncat.
Fence! Same fence. Yep. Same fence.
Yep. High. Yep. Yep. Strong. Yep.
God. God, rip same fence. God,
schnauzer down same fence. No? Cat,
now: catfeet spookaway fence: spring:
cat flies: cat balances on top. Me: dig.
Dog dig, did dig, do dig, doubledig.
Now . . . underground now . . . fence.
Piss on same, on fence, on fencepost.
Me: I mark this. This is mine.

—Nietzsche

Sidney Wade

Dog Sonnet

I know where I'm going
Plutarch's coming with
Off to goof drobble sproing
Snoop a rich double whiff
Fish kill at the sink hole
O magnificent luck
Grabble pute marly roll
In the turrible druck
Hey a mole wholly rapture
Dig it four paw full blown
Wait a minute got fleas
Got to stickle the flap
Of this ear here's a bone
Prone to me. Sneeze.

—*Gracie*

Lawrence Raab

Katie's Words

Outside. Field. Food,
of course, *Dog* and *walk*
and *sit*. These you're sure
I understand. Like
my name. And yours. *Good*
and *bad*. Not always
the difference. Or so
you'd say, mistaking
what I know for how
I choose to act,
confusing the word
and its effect. You
raise your voice and I
consent. More often
than not. Stay or come.
Go to my place.
And if I'd rather
be off by myself
chasing a squirrel
or rolling around
in some interesting
smell, I know freedom
isn't everything.

And so do you. Speak,
you say, and I have.
Enough is enough.
I think it's time
for a walk, to sniff
around for a while,
scratch at the snow, dig
a hole just to see
if anything's there.

—*Katie*

George Minot

Down

Tell me don't ask me
and let's get going.
No I'm not grinning
but grimace yes I guess
showing against my lifted black rubber lip
my pink gum and cracked old tooth,
but there's no snarl behind it
like my gravelly growl,
only me
and I am the fieldy world
full of its sensualities
to nose through
gliding in my handsome coat my loyal law,
roots and carcasses to dig.
A replacement rock to carry home
is better than no bone
and heavy it hangs my head I bite it.
I hear you.
I answer you, I move.
I smell all mixed meaningful messages.
Except in sexy sleep there's no division.
We don't think,
we know and go.

The answer's in our eyes,
pond-dark pools with white day whites:
Of course we dream:
in all we do.
And you think we love you,
and we do.

—*Jason*

$_{Roy}$ Blount, Jr.

A Country Dog in the City
(On a Leash, Which Is Bizarre Enough)
Comes Upon an Obedience Class:
Twelve Dogs and Their Masters
Walking Around in a Circle

Well
If that
don't beat
all.

Don't they smell

SQUIRREL!

    SQUIRREL!

SQUIRREL!

—Molly

Jennifer Allen

A War Poem

In die time auf Hilda
    das Hill vas Hilda's
        zu roam, pillage, ravage, plunder
            grass und sage,
            bird und snake,
            fire und quake.
            Nay, nein, nothing stopped Hilda.
    "Come, Hilda, Come!"
        das hu-manns roared.
    Bah, hah, yah,
        sang Hilda.
    Wenn hu-mann say, "Hilda, Come!"
    Hilda v-run.

In die time auf Hilda
    alle crimes led zu Hilda.
    Hilda,
        pure-bred blue-blood dog-dog;
        barked barked über canyon alle nacht long,
        nailed neighbor's
        poodle's ears zu lawn, chewed turtle und shell.
    Hilda,
        born auf big-balled Adolph;

tipped trash can, chased skunk, raid milk-man
rack.

Hilda,

    master auf alle masters;
    ate squid, chewed pelican, shat beach rat.

In die time auf Hilda

  Hilda did vhat Hilda vant.

    Hilda stood

    battle-axe broad,

    short-hair sleek,

    clipped-tail sharp,

    surveying neighbor's Jap garten yard.

  Hilda see alle.

    See water, waffer, wafferfall.

    See fish, fifch, fifchergrund.

    See fish-full Hilda playgrund.

  Hilda point.

  Hilda watch fifch

    swim, swam, swum

        über rivers

            unten bridges

                nieder waffer falls.

  Hilda trap fifch mit paw.

  Hilda bite waffer, eat waffer, cough.

  Hilda take flapping, floundering fifch auf mouth,

carry fifch zu Hilda lawn,
                drop fifch,
                        re-treat zu garten, re-peat
                        z-attack, re-turn zu Hilda lawn.
        Wenn Jap garten vas nihilismus und
                every fifch vas auf Hilda lawn,
Hilda sit. Hilda stay. Hilda proud.

In die time auf Hilda
        das hu-manns shout, "No, Hilda, No!"
                Das hu-manns take fisch, fisch, fisch, fisch,
                fisch.
                Das hu-manns v-run mit fisch, fisch, fisch,
                fisch, fisch.
        Die Hilda follow.
        Das humans drop fifch in waffer in Hilda (purgatory-
        post-skunk-laundry-room) sink.
                Die Hilda growl
                Das fifch dead.
                Das hu-manns shout "$$$$$$$!"
                Die Hilda bark.

In die time auf Hilda
        eine ding frighten Hilda:
                cap gun.
                        Eine old bathrobed
                                fifchwife auf Jap garten
                                        owned cap gun.

Wenn Hilda vas

fifch-fat fed auf Hilda lawn,

fifchwife came wading up,

nein net, nein reel, nein hook,

eine cap gun pop

got Hilda zu

jump,

bark,

v-run

very, very, very far.

—*Hilda Guard*

Natalie Kusz

Nights, the house grows larger, open
floor widening toward gray
indistinct walls. Here, then, I find
the cotton rabbit lying still—
one plush foot stretching long on the carpet.
I leap in, bite, fling it wide
and follow, pursuing now,
no muzzle to hold me
from catching it, catching it.

—Julio

Noy Holland

Alice

Let the rest play step
and fetch and shake and
kiss when bidden. *Chew!*
Do you?
I hawk and gobble, gone
over the bony field.
I belly flop, I clear the pond
of ducks and sticks and rubble,
dive. See? See?
Leggy me.
Off the bed!
In your house!
Out of the kitchen!
Really? Oh,
really? Oh, gimme
a ride in your ragtop I'll
let you love my spotty tum.

—*Alice*

Padgett Powell

Full Neurological Work-up

Patient: Spode
Breed: Pit Bull
Symptoms: Partial paralysis
Remarks: Full neurological work-up indicated in absence of organic damage

Rorshach Section

blot #1

Patient response: Dead cat.

blot #2

Patient response: Dead cat.

blot #3

Patient response: That? [considers] Dead cat.

blot #4

Patient response: That one? Hmm. Hmmm. Tough one.

Investigator: Please, sir. Spontaneity is—

Patient response: Dead cat.

Remarks: Nonaberrant.

—*Spode*

Cynthia Heimel

Sally

I am big, I am gigantic, look at me way up here
Perched on the back of the sofa
Wearing my invisible tiara
A huge bat-eared ten-pound monarch Papillon,
Head right next to my human.
My human and I are a celestial duo
Commitment clinched on our first night,
My wet little three-month puppy nose pressed to her neck
We became one.
She loves me best in all the whole world.
Better than big black Doc, he protects us, thinks he's big, hah
Better than sofa-boy Homer with his Harrod's snooty collar, oh
         please spare me.
Better than Mike and Digby the kissy thugs who scrabble at her
         face, so unseemly, so lacking in my perfect regal dignity
(Okay so I eat cat poop sometimes, but delicately with panache),
Better than that pretender, that backyard bred Josie
With her submissive wiggle who's she kidding
Josie pushes me off my pillow at night Josie must die,
My human is mine, for I am descended from Marie Antoinette's
         Mimi.

                                             —*Sally*

Merrill Markoe

Lewis Describes His Day

It's 5 A.M. I'm wide awake so to your bed I race.
Won't you please get up and shove some groceries in my face?
Now I head outside and dig big holes in your backyard.
Then I race back in and eat a pillow and some lard.
Next I jump into your pool. Then roll around in mud.
Then I have sex with your couch to prove I'm still a stud.
Hook me to the leash and let me pull you into trees.
I will gasp and choke and then I'll knock you to your knees.
Let me get the garbage down and dive on it with glee.
Let me kiss you. Just a second. Let me get this flea.
Oh boy. There's my dinner. Aw, it's just the same old goo.
Give me all your food instead or I will drool on you.
All I want to do is sit right on you and be near you.
Ask me to do anything. I'll act like I can't hear you.
Come and wrestle with me. If you don't I'll show you how.
Then I must have all your food, so give it to me now.

—*Lewis*

Mark Richard

Y'All Are Bird Dogs, Aren't You?

*To Bullette and Katie, the blue-speckled bitch-hounds who pushed me out of
the back of the truck and broke my leg on the Uncertain Ranch.*

Lean way out, y'all said.
Stand on the tool box
And lean WAY out, y'all said.

This thaw
Up North
Billions of juicy birds
WAY out
Where you can walk
On beautiful
Pond ice.

—*Ray*

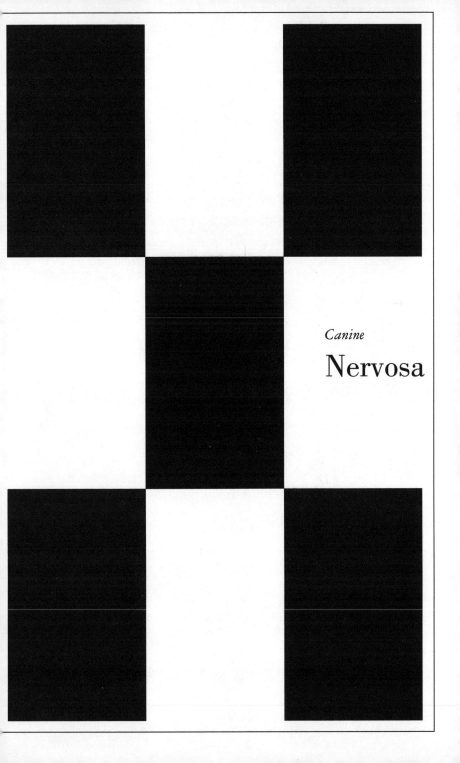

Canine
Nervosa

Arthur Miller

Lola's Lament

I worry.
I have to because nobody else does.
Some strange car comes up the driveway—
They go right on talking. They trust,
I don't. Threat crosses my nose
Twenty times a day.
No wonder I bark and menace,
Who knows who it could be at the door
'Specially in these times.

Walk in the woods with them
You'd never know they're passing
Under two tremendous owls perched way up,
Or stepping on fresh coyote piss
Or a hair of an elderly rat on a blade of grass
Or the spunk of rutting deer last night,
Or the rubbing of a bear, God forbid,
On a bent birch beside the path.

So I worry.
Sleep with my ears up, not soundly.
When I'm not watching I'm greeting.
People are not grateful enough
For visitors. I am. I worry
About them not being grateful enough.
So I make up for it by howling
Till they get up off the couch
To shake hands. Between the dangers
And the greetings I'm simply exhausted.

—Lola

Terese Svoboda

Cosmo Dog

The way all girl dogs talk French you'd think we
lapped wine and jumped hoops only in Paree.

But non. We are simply cats trapped in dogs,
trans-special, soon to travel to Den Haag

or somewhere with specialists (a species-ist)
who can free us from both this Gaulist

lisp and this dreadful bark for which I think
they call us bitch. Twice I've consulted shrinks

on the subject of my name, to wit: Spot.
Run, Spot, run? they hmmm. Think TV, think spot

on primetime, you're an actress for Milkbone
who never contemplates drinking cologne.

But it's "Out, damned Spot" over and over,
I sigh. At least they used a good author.

—_Spot_

Pearson **Marx**

Hugs

A Threnody

Hugs! Hugs! Damn these hugs!
It's the price I pay for being loved.
Just when I've finished a bowl of my grub
She comes lurching toward me—
Wanting to hug.

Hugs! Hugs! I feel stalked.
It's the price I pay for my daily walks.
Just when I'm playing, chasing a fly
She comes creeping toward me—
That look in her eye.

Hugs! Hugs! She won't leave me alone!
It's the price I pay for my rawhide bones.
Just when I'm cozy, curled up on the bed
She's lying on top of me—
I'd rather be dead.

—Josephine

Elise Paschen

Sam's Ghazals

You're out. The house is dead. With me:
you're safe. Why not stay home, instead, with me?

That Ur prince whisked you off past four.
At my leash-end, you're not misled by me.

He's like a tide. He comes. He goes.
I'm always here. Life's anchored with me.

My needs are few: a bowl, a lead, some love.
You won't get in the red with me.

You never have to cook, just pop a Mighty Dog:
a snap to have breakfasted with me.

He paws, he yaps, he barely listens.
I'm all ears. Much is left unsaid with me.

Maybe I have my quirks (stairs scare, streets clank),
but you've always kept your head with me.

He is six foot one. I am one foot high.
Don't ever let him tread on me.

Though small, I claim my space and like you snug.
(It's tough sharing a bed with me.)

My name is Samson. Yours is Paschen.
So keep your name and stay unwed with me.

—*Sam*

Lab Lines

Retrieving is uncertain work.
Fetch him bright fragrant feathers dead,
He grins and pats his gratitude.
But barf a scented toad beside his bed,
He screams, slams doors and me.

A still warm, gay and bloody duck,
He kneels and gathers like a grail.
But bring up week-old possum warm,
His voice goes grim; his face turns pale.
It's all retrieval; reactions vary.

Balls or bumpers, birds and toads,
I think it should be none or all.
Last night I urped a knot of tennis net;
Picky bastard won't ever get the ball.
I'm keeping the next duck too.

—*Jessie*

Ralph Lombreglia

Daisy, Five, Speaks to Sophia, Two

I was here first.
I'm the real baby.
In a former life, it was me
who was cute, cute, cute.
When she went to have you,
she carried my picture to focus
on when her labor got bad.
She hasn't taken my picture since.
Where's your gold fur, newcomer?
Where's your tail?

You get everything. Stuffed teddies
I'm mauling if I see my chance,
a Barbie utterly
incorrect for your age,
trips to Burger King I can
smell a mile away. You drop
Barbie's shoes when he
lifts you from the car,
and the man who once
threw me sticks
till his arm fell off
now paws black sidewalk snow
for Barbie's absurd high heels.

Food. You get all the food.
You sashay this house with
boneless breast in your fists,
bacon strips and string cheese
woven through your fingers.
You get steak. You get eggs.
I get kibble. He says,
"The only philosophically defensible position is vegetarianism"
While he gnaws the bones of birds!
All I want is a stick.
A stick and some chicken.
Some chicken and a stick.

When they fight, I hide
in the downstairs half-bath
with the moldy wallpaper.
I get as much of my body as
possible onto the oval rug.
Yes, you should hide too, but
find your own place.
This is a small room and
you get bigger all the time.
What in this vast and
exquisitely smelly world
do they fight about?
I know, you don't know.
It gives me an unquenchable
thirst for toilet water,
but they've left the seat down.

And you're sitting on it.
Could you take your foot off my head?
Anything to eat in those pockets?
Off! I am not a horsey.
You *do* know how to lift the toilet seat!
Let me just clamber up
for a long cool one. Whoops!
There goes Barbie.
And here come the tears.
Don't cry, stepsister.
It hurts my ears. Dogs
don't cry. True, we don't
laugh much, either,
but we're famous, or
at least my breed is famous (and it's
the other reason people like us,
besides the good-with-children thing)
for our smiles.

—Daisy

Abigail Thomas

Doggerel

I'm quintessential female
I have a jealous heart
and that last girl he brought up here
was nothing but a tart

she ate up all his ice cream
she drank up all his schnapps
and then she made a noisy fuss
when I climbed on their laps

he took me off the sofa
he put me in the chair
she said, "My god, your furniture
is nothing but dog-hair"

(my master is an idiot
how freely I admit it
he used to have a thinking-cap
but someone must have hid it)

she laughed at all his silly jokes
(which most girls find a chore)
and then she took off all her clothes
and dropped them on the floor

it's not that I'm small-minded
he's had some other lovers
but this one didn't understand
I sleep under the covers

I don't like to be pushed around
I do not care for scowls
she told him that I snapped at her
when all I did was growl

I'm certainly no prude
(I could prove this if he'd let me)
but I saw no reason why she shouldn't
rue the day she met me

her clothes I chewed to pieces
her silly boots I bit up
some of this mess I swallowed
but most of it I spit up

"How could you keep a dog like him?"
she cried, "this filthy cur?"
my master looked at me and smiled,
"No, not a him, a her."

—*Suzy*

Jeanne Schinto

Stalker

I can't figure it out:
You don't seem alarmed by the man who has followed us here
from our last address.
How did he find us?

It is the same guy, isn't it?
The door to his vehicle, being closed,
sounds the same. The clothing, the same.
The footsteps on the porch, the same.

Well, sort of the same . . .

But you never let the hulk in,
so I can't tell for sure.

Tell me: What does he want?

I bark and growl and paw the glass (I tore the curtain once).
My hackles are spindles. And you?

You come blithely down the stairs
and pick up off the floor what he's left you,
paper pushed through the slot.
You look it over, then you tear it apart.
And I can only wait for another chance to do the same to him,
tomorrow.

—Jazz

Karen Shepard

Glom: Labrador, 110 pounds

What?
What?
What?
It *was* broken—

I'm a detective without clues.
I'm ready to help.
Now they're angry.
I slink upstairs. They follow.
I press myself into corners.
Things fall down.
Later they're singing.
I lie low.

They leave. Strangers spend the night.
They come back.
The suitcase stays out.
Yesterday: possums. Right outside.

I'm sleeping. I'm punished.
A biscuit. They rub my ears.
They point.
Something's held before my nose.
Not food.

Fool. Dim bulb. Big galoot.
Glom.
Pinhead.
Birch: I'm named for a tree.
At times they say it like *Walk.*
At times they say it like *Bad.*

They laugh. Go on to something else.
I try a yawn. Lick my paws.
Hear my name.
Watch their eyes:
Emergency instructions. Foreign language.

—*Birch*

Lee Smith

In the Heat of the Night

My biological clock is ticking.
The time has come.
Soon I will be in heat.

Heat! O what is it
that they speak of
with such horror
in hushed voices over wine?

Heat!
My mind runs to Huskies,
to a big strong Husky from the north
with pale eyes and hot breath
his underbelly white and soft as snow.

Not to mention
macho Boxers,
Standard Poodles,
Collies, Chows,
Airedales flying through the windows,
German Shepherds,
lots of Labs.

I am not even afraid of Rottweilers.

Heat!
I have big dreams.
Eleven puppies,
Maybe more.
I will lie on a blanket in the shade
of a tree nursing puppies.
The more I give
The more I will be fulfilled.

Heat!
O but they intervene.
They want me to love only them.
Only them!
(Not my species, not my kind.)

I will become a decorator dog
from the pages of L.L. Bean.
I will walk beside them every evening
down the long lane of their middle age.
I will chase sticks and balls.
I will lick them.
But O! There is no big Husky
under this pale moon.

—Gracie

Mary Morris

Missing: A Dog's Doggerel

Part of me is missing.
I woke to find it so.
Part of me is missing.
I've searched from head to toe.

I've looked in every corner
And climbed on every chair.
But part of me is missing.
I've looked and it's not there.

I cannot understand this.
Before I was intact.
Now I'm somehow altered.
This is just a fact.

I'm hungry as I've been.
I sniff just like before.
But I have been diminished
There's less of me, not more.

I fear there's something missing.
I used to be complete.
Now I find I am indifferent
When a bitch walks by in heat.

Perhaps they've made me human.
It's how humans seem to me.
Seeking, looking, searching
For what can never be.

—*Snowball*

+ *Andrew* Hudgins

Buddy

I'll just stand here till you notice me, sir.

Sir, I'm still standing here. Still just standing.
Just standing and waiting for you to notice me.

Excuse me, sir. I need to, you know, uh . . .

It's hard to put this into words. I mean
so bluntly, sir.
       I need to void myself.
There, I've said it. I hope you're happy now,
now that I've been so rude, indelicate.
Now that I've had to humiliate myself.

Sir, I've got to urinate.
       I've got to pee.

I'm going to piss like an open hydrant—please!

Oh, bless you, sir. Oh bless you, bless you, bless you—
and please don't let the screen door spank my bottom.

—Buddy

+ *Danny* Anderson

Domi Solus

The house gives way to dimmer shades of dim
As tree limbs quiver and a passing storm
Unloads its tantrum as I wait for him.
Although I've often promised my reform
I've rifled through his freshly laundered socks,
Played "sliders" on the Oriental rug,
Shredded tissues, and tipped the litter box.
The cat, my Super Ego, waxes smug
At all the mischief I cannot repair,
And snakes her tail high on the mantelpiece.
As always, after rage there comes despair.
Outside dark starlings ride the wind's increase;
The cold rainwater trickles from the eaves
While I sink low and watch the trembling leaves.

—*Virgil*

Substance
Abuse

+ *Erin* McGraw

Drunk Dog

The floor tilts. I'm trying to go tell Him
the floor tilts, but I'm having trouble
because the floor tilts. Twice now walls
have slipped. I want to tell Him about
the walls and the floor and also the smear
of guacamole on His ankle.
But it's hard to make much progress when
the floor keeps buckling under you
and sometimes—this is sensational!—
there are six of Him. His smell
has gotten huge. It's as big
as the underside of garbage cans,
where, in heaven, I'll sniff forever.
The floor slams up into my snout
and I lose sight of Him, but not
His smell, so rich and smellable.
It pulls me to Him, where I say,
"The floor tilts," but it comes out strange.

He laughs, looks down, and pushes me
out the back door; my rump lands hard.
Though I'm not sure, the ground seems to tilt
here too. I'll tell Him when He comes back.
The air is full of cats and sirens.
I bring up supper, then chase fireflies.
Snap, snap. They drift above my nose,
up toward the windows. Snap. Snap, snap.

—Stickerdog

Lynda Barry

I love my master I love my master

God I love my master
Of all the dogs I have the best master
What a great master
Yes I can get on the bed Yes I can have
A bite of her brownie Oh No it's a
Pot brownie oh god I am so high
She is starting to look very weird to me
So much skin so much open skin on her so bald all over
I want to smell her mmmmmmaster mmmmmmaster
She's laughing at me quit laughing at me
Now she's barfing now who is laughing
Har Har Har Master oh no now I'm barfing
She thinks there was LSD in the brownie
He is laughing
Now I am outside for biting the Boyfriend
I hate
The Boyfriend
Now I am outside
There was LSD in that brownie

Maintain maintain

Please let me back in Master I am

Riding on a really bad trip Master

Please Master Please Baldy

Before I eat garbage

Before I bite car tires

Master I need to come in

Before I go over to Pepe's yard and

Tempt him with my LSD barking

Hey Pepe Pepe Har har har rawo rawo rawo

Oh No Pepe is not attached to his chain!

Running running steps steps steps PLEASE MASTER PLEASE

PLEASE OH NO PLEASE

Door opens Thank You Master I love you Master what

A good Master

The Boyfriend says he is too high to look at me

He agrees

There was LSD in that brownie

He got it from his neighbor

She wants to go to the hospital

He says she'll come down in a minute

All our jaws are tight and we want to bite each other so bad

My jaws are killing me this is worse

Than the chocolate mescaline from last week that made

Me just want to hump her
My Beautiful Master
If you think she looks good now
You should see her on mesc.
GOD I HATE THE SOUND OF THIS COLLAR
MASTER GET THIS OFF ME MASTER WHERE ARE YOU GOING
The Boyfriend wants to hear The Doors
Don't play The Doors on acid. Not that man's voice on acid. No.
I will freak. I will bite. Maintain maintain
I will lay on the floor I will close my eyes
Oh no I see too many of Pepe's heads
I see mange
I see cans of Skippy Dog Food
Cans and cans of Skippy Dog Food swirling
Flashing I'm peaking
Don't think about Skippy
Don't think about Pepe
Think calm thoughts. Calm ones.
Master. Mmmmmmaster.
Master wants to hold me Master wants to hold me
Come here boy come here
Get Him Off The Bed says the Boyfriend says the Freakster
Get Him Off Because I'm Freaking
This Is Very Bad Acid says the Master

I Need to Hold Him to Maintain says the Master
Mmmmmaster
And when her fingers touch under my chin
And when her fingers undo my collar
I am blissed out.
I lick her fingers
The Boyfriend says he hates me
And has always hated me
The Boyfriend is starting to confess
Everything
I look into the Master's green eyes
They are getting larger and larger

Now it is later. The Boyfriend is gone.
The Master says he is a fag
Good riddance she is crying
I lick her face
We are coming down
Our jaws ache and itch
Finally she falls asleep and then I fall asleep
And somewhere
The fag boyfriend falls asleep
Fag boyfriend if you are ever reading this
I thank you with all of my heart

I thank you for the righteous brownies
And I thank you for confessing when you were high on acid
That you fucked Vicky
And Stacy
And Angela
And that you are not really sure
If girls turn you on.
Girls turn me on
Thank you Boyfriend thank you sir
Now you are outside forever
I love my Master I love my Master
God I love my Master
Of all the dogs
I know
I love my Master
best.

—*Bob Barker*

Bob Barker (the dog) and Me (the lady)
I am still kicking. Bob's last kick was
in the summer of 1986.

+ *Andrew* **Hudgins**

Rosie

Feet and butthole. I love
his feet and butthole. Well,
his butthole most of all.
And his dangler when he front-
humps Mistress. (I know, it
looks crazy to me too.)
Then his dangler smells
magnificent. Pungent
and almost gamey, but
not as great as his butthole.
Nothing's great as buttholes.
But still it's pretty fine,
that dangler, and you think
he'd be proud of it, happy
to have it sniffed thoroughly,
but he yelps and swats at me.
Of course, I love that dangler
and want to roll on it
—who wouldn't?—but it's not as great
as his butthole, which is full,
full of dark wonders, fragrant,
almost as good as a dog's
butthole, almost as great

as the place near the river
where I somersaulted on
a soft, rank fish last August
—perfume!—and got smacked
and washed, and where I still
check every day because
it might return. It could.
And I rubbed my snout on it
and somersaulted on it
like I'd like to somersault
on his butthole, but he's embarrassed.
I don't know why. Nothing's
as great as a good butthole
and all buttholes are good. Great!

—Rosie

Bernard Cooper

A Toast to the Cook

A long fragrant leash of steam
tethers me to your figure
stirring a pot at the stove. Herbs steep,
earthy and engrossing
as the dirt I dig in my dreams.
A tracery of ancient spills
rises from the carpet fiber: bland, innumerable
crumbs of bread; a whiff of stale
table wine, once so wet
and full and sweet, now a stubborn
russet stain. Mouldering scraps
reek from the pail, vibrant as the morning news.
Cold coffee grounds glow
in my head like embers.
Distracting odors slough from your hand
as you bend down and reach for me—
the soup you sampled and
wiped from your lips; ghostly cloves
of garlic. A tangled, enticing
maze of decay

spreads from your breath
when you say my name.
I lift my nose—a toast to the cook—
and sniff your incomparable crotch,
a banquet of spoor.

—Zachary

Rescue

Natalie Kusz

Retired Greyhound, II

Leaning into you now, my dark head
seeking your hand, your leg
stumbling back from the force of me,
I could almost forget that other time—the deep
men's voices I shudder at even now, the raised
hands I still fear—almost, not quite.
No, if I lost that era, my very
healed bones would dream it, the way

those scars around your eyes speak their own
perpetual history: the size and depth
of a dog's mouth, the tearing
great fear of a child.
We will never outrace these, our grief
and our knowledge, but here
in this wide expanse of yard, the dragonflies
scooping down around us, we can lean
in and perceive ourselves, you and I: the astonishing
exceptions among our kinds.

—Julio

R. S. Jones

Shelter

You paused outside
to look into my cage.
I tried to play it right
wanting to catch your eye
with a shy glint in my own,
      a soft bark,
that said, "Choose me,"
in a canine grammar
I hoped you'd understand.

Your face held nothing
(Pity, maybe)
that let me believe
you would ever want
a dog like me.

You turned once,
twice,
a hundred times,
coming and going
the length of my cage.
(Coming and going

like you do now,
ten times a day.)
Then walked away.

I could not stand another day of
strangers coming to stare.
Passing me over for younger dogs who
knew too little to have the strange
        look of longing
I could not keep from my eyes.

I could not stand another night
alone in that place
        the cracked cement floor
        the howls and whines that kept me sleepless
(Did you know that sound is still the one I hear
when you wake me kicking from dreams
sleeping in your bed?)

Then suddenly you were back.
I saw you glance at the card
hung onto my gate—
        a false name, a date of arrival,
otherwise a blank
        no age, no history,
        nothing,
that would stay with you forever
and never go.

You leaned your face into the fence
curling your hand through the wires,
        blinking in the sun.
(Neither one of us so young
in the bright, Spring light
yet wanting to be.)

I let one paw
hover in the air
but looked away,
not wanting to show my eagerness,
        but wanting
to find a way to tell you
that I would be a good dog
and how much I wanted to be owned.
(A dog is only half himself
without a master.
Unfinished, half-alive)

I could not move
        nor speak
but when you dropped to your knees
and reached two fingers towards my fur

I felt myself fall,
(oh god I could not help myself)
letting my body form the words
head back, eyes closed
throat exposed,
legs flailing in the air.
"Please," I said. "Yes, please.
Take me. Yes."

—Scout

Honor Moore

Runaway

It's dark, almost foggy, the first day
I've seen what they call snow. I leap up—
wire—it's a see-through trick. I fall,
leap again, shout. Down, up, shout harder.
That's when I see her first, tall Hover
doing what they call love: at my ears,
white star, black silk rippling like grass
in summer wind. We take what she calls
walk—cold road in winter morning dark.
The sadness she has, I feel it all.

Run! Smell! Snort! Out of jail! Hover laughs.
Sniff! Dance! Squirrel up a tree! Hover's
scared I'll run. Snort! Skunk smell and squirrel!
I'm feet up the tree, claws in, then back
on the road galloping. Dark fog, crack
of ice, snow falling. Hover walks, I'm
running. If I spoke words, I'd tell her
how I lost everything I had.
Truck came, I ran. Fear, woods, no mother—
weasel smell! deer!—no sister or brother . . .

Back to the flat place and no blue car,
no popcorn, Big Mac, child smell or smoke.
Gone for good I'm sure when the night stick
yanks me into wire place of dog-
fright smell, leap-longing, yelp of prayer.
Shove of food under wire for days
before Hover wants me, gate's unlocked,
and I dream Grandfather nips old air,
rests back on his haunches. We walk, she
calls like a song, but it's in me—hell

snarl of Mack truck smell, whir of mad eye
on, off, scrape of monstrous metal chin
digging at road ice. So scared I lose
other sound. Hover's feet are running,
but I'm disappeared. Hideous screech,
roar cutting at my cold black heels.
Drive of hard wire, night stick, terror
smell of coyote and bobcat. For
the first time I feel snow. Far away
Hover cries. My fast feet forget her.

Wood smell, snow smell, fast trail of deer smell,
even wolf smell. Something pulling me
forward from a long past, ancestors
or knowledge. Moon, circle of eaters,
burn smell, smoke, bones, and we are dancing,
food thrown as we creep toward the fire,
laugh of our teeth in the bright darkness.
So much calls to me it's night before
I remember song shout, tall Hover,
the smell she promised was mine alone.

—Brussels

Gordon Lish

Rusty

My name is Rusty.
I was Gordon's dog for fourteen years.
He went one summer
off to Brant Lake Camp
and while
he was gone
his mother and dad
did
away
with
me.
To save him
having to see
nature do it.
Or so they said.
Anyway, nature didn't do it.
Actually, it turned out
human nature decided to do it.
But that's probably
the same nature in its fashion.
Speaking of which,
I was a Welsh terrier,
and was enjoying a certain vogue

at the time.
Truth be known, I believe
myself to have been
a tremendous hit
with Gordon.
You might
say I was,
for the time that I was,
the life in his life.
Hell, the song in him you could
even go so far as to maybe say.
Not just cut-up
prose
for the sake of a cut-up dog
in a cut-and-paste book
for a C-note of a fee
and one more fucking proof
of a grown-up human being
at his
natural mongrel perfidies.

—Rusty

Rick **Bass**

The Odyssey

An Excerpt

We are hounds. We have always been hounds. The long-ago faceless people-Before dumped us roadside in Mississippi. There were three of us, all females. We must have had an energy even then. The one sister got hit by a truck that just kept going. We stayed by her on the roadside and watched her not get up. There wasn't anywhere else to go. Then his old truck came, the next day, or the next. Driving slower. An old dull-colored thing. It was the color of old red clay.

It was spring and he was driving slow to keep from hitting the box turtles that come out of the earth at that time.

We had mange and ticks and fleas and worms, which is I suppose why the long-ago faceless people-Before dumped us. Perhaps they had children around the house. Perhaps . . .

He drove past, going way around our sister, and we jumped
out and ran down the road after him, barking, wobbling on short
legs. We had not done that to other trucks and cars that passed.
I don't know why we did it to him.

He was weak, had not ever owned a dog before. He was going
to keep going.

We must have known he was weak,
is why we chased him. It's hard to remember.
He looked in the mirror and saw Ann, fat little Ann,
jump out of the weeds and run down the road after him.
Easy Ann.
He stopped and backed the truck up.
He was a do-gooder, I could tell that.
He was going to take us to the pound,
a place all dogs know about in their hearts.
I jumped out of the weeds and
ran down the road after Ann,
barking at her to come back, to wait for a better one.
We were living in an old ratty house
the color of a buzzard's neck.
The old house was back in the high green weeds,
set up on cinder blocks to let
snakes and wildcats and rodents
pass beneath it.

We lived in the back room on the south side,
in what had once been the kitchen.
We went to the bathroom on old
newspapers and magazines in a corner bedroom.
It was a big house, all the doors and
windows busted out, and it listed
like a ship about to go out to sea,
or about to slide to the bottom of the sea.
He got Ann. He picked her up.
Delighted, she immediately rolled over on her back and began
peeing, which is why she is called Peeing Ann,
a golden fountain in the spring sunlight,
in Mississippi,
pee of happiness.

He hadn't ever *touched* a dog before;
didn't know what to do. Stood there
and held her, waiting for the pee to run out.
I barked shrill and wild, a puppy, snapping at his ankles.
Trying to get him to give her back.
He tried to pick me up with his free hand
but couldn't, I dodged and twisted, yapped
though I am not a yapping dog. I am a hound.
He took Ann back to his truck, put
her on that awful littered floorboard,
then came back for me.
I ran into the woods and hid.
When he kept coming—crawling under the rusting barbed wire fence,
catching his shirt on it
—*Good heart* I thought quickly, examining him in my mind for the first time—
I ran up the steps, into that rotting old mansion.
He kept coming. I hid in a slumping down closet.

The back door had been blown off
by a hurricane
or a tornado
or any of a thousand other sheer malevolent bad lucks
that roamed through the Mississippi woods.

He's not smart. He searched quickly through
the house,
Thinking, I could hear, "A pair would be nice,
they ought not to be split up."

When he came to the place
where the door had been blown away,
he assumed I had leapt off the porch
into the brambles far below, into that great void.
He underestimated me.
He expected the least of me.
He wrote me off, sold me off and out
But still I love him.

He went back to his truck, that hideous old death trap.
I could hear him thinking, "At least I saved one."
I could hear him thinking, "That one would have been too wild,
anyway."
I heard him drive away.
It was an awful kind of loneliness, when he was gone:
He and Ann.
The woods grew larger.
Light seemed suddenly to get sucked out of the old house; it
slumped further.

I crawled out from under the old newspapers
and went out to the road where my other sister, the one-who-
remained, still
was. He didn't take that one away.
　　　　I sat there to keep the buzzards away, and waited,
though I didn't know what for.
After a while, I could hear him thinking,
about five or six miles up the road,
thinking guilty thoughts,
thinking, "I didn't try hard enough."
The awfulness of what he had done—
taking my Ann!—
beginning to settle heavy on him
like a slumping house.
He came driving back.
When he came around the bend, I ran at his truck, barking,
but when he got out of it again
I ran back under the fence, through the weeds,
and into the shack—but this time I willed him to catch me.

He's not bright. He made the same mistake.
Went to the same door, the same torn-off one,
and stared down into the bramble-maw.
Figured I was wilder than wild,
and left. Again.

Now my dog-heart was flattened.
I went back out to the road,

even before he had driven out of sight
But he didn't see me.
He was busy looking down at the floorboard,
admiring Ann,
who was on her back, thumping her tail,
and who had begun to pee again.

But he came back a third time,
saw me sitting by the roadside again,
at the edge of the tall weeds,
in the heat rising from the black road in waves,
and chased me once more.

He figured out that I was not leaping into that void each time,
and he stalked the whole house instead,
like a detective, and this time
he found me, in there under all those papers,
as if I had been birthed from that rotting old house,
as if the trash and papers were my afterbirth.
That was almost ten years ago.
Of course I wonder about the Ones-Before-Him,
What it would have been like, with them.
I suspect they were deer hunters.
We would have been only two in a pack of fifty,
chasing deer through the night,
baying on silver nights
frost nights,
baying hard on the heels of antlered deer
running wild like kings through the forest . . .
No.
The other master, the one-before,
was weak and cowardly and coal-hearted.
He would have used us for bait on his trotline
He would have made us fight in pits with spiked collars.

He took Ann and me over to his girlfriend's, Elizabeth's.
They fed us watery milk from a bowl
on the back porch of her house
with the cows lowing out in the field
and the blue dusk sliding in from the bayou below:

the groans of cows in the spring,
and then the night, the fireflies, this new world.
We slept in a big shoebox with our bellies warm and full,
round and drum tight, snoring, slobbering in our happiness.
And though they had never had dogs before
they did not take us to the pound.
What dog knows its parents, anyway?

I am the Alpha and the Homer.
I am a female, spayed so I will live longer,
and I am loyal, the faithful Homer-Dog,
named for another orphan, Homer Wells.
The more feckless Ann gets,
the more loyal I must become, to balance her sloppiness.
She walks right through mud puddles.
She farts;
I never fart.
Ann takes big dumps
wherever and whenever she feels like it.
I go into the woods
and hunker behind a tree.
I am modest; I am loyal.
          We are twins.
Children are the only ones who can tell us apart.
They know things: we like being in their company.
Ann licks them, slobbers their sweet faces with kisses,
even when she has been out eating cow pies.

She pretends not to understand the command, "No licking,"
just as she pretends to be too dense
to understand "No farts."
I wonder about the one who's not here,
the third one,
what she would have been like.
By now it is clearly established
that I am the Number One Dog,
the Ultimate Dog, the best.

He quit his job not long after he rescued us.
And we liked this. He was home all the time, then:
       the three of us.
He carried each of us in his arms,
one in each arm, like a loaf of bread, or a football,
and we went for long walks,
beneath spring-green canopies of light,
past old barns, past cattle, past muddy ponds and
buzzards, herons, and skunks; hay fields.
Hot. It was always hot,
in Mississippi.

I am the Alpha and the Homer,
but things always happen to me,
never to Ann, who, despite her gracelessness,
has the slippery luck of a fish,
and glides or blunders through things untouched.

   Once I was running hard,
running fast, young, running strong just
to feel my speed. I ran through a
pile of pecan leaves, head high: I aimed to just
burst through their midst.
   But there was a stone wall hidden
in their midst. I hit it going about ninety miles per hour
and cartwheeled, limp, knocked out.
They thought I was dead. But Ann licked my face, revived me.
We were not even two years old.
I walked in circles for hours, staggering. A concussion.
I hit the wall first because
I was fastest and best. Ann was
waddling along behind me and when
she saw me smack that hidden wall, she had veered off.
   I don't know this for sure but
I think I am older than she is, by a minute or two.

After he quit his job and was
just living out on the farm
like a bozo, just
writing, instead of doing muscle-work,
he got poor quick,
and when it came time for our annual
worming, to save money he didn't
take us to the vet but instead tried to do it himself.

He saved two dollars by buying horse-worming pills—
Big blue gel-caps the size of garden slugs,
filled with turpentine.
I went first
because I was, and am, the loyal one;
because I came first when he called,
just slightly ahead of Ann.

   We were in the sunroom sitting up on the old iron bed late in
the afternoon. The room was filled with golden light. The last
light I would ever see, it almost turned out.
   He put me up on the bed like he was a real vet instead of a
fuck-up; as if it were an examining table. He held my muzzle
skyward and tried to slip that giant blue slug-pill down my
throat.

I panicked, and gagged;
I chomped down on it,
punctured it with my teeth.

It was a horse-sized portion.
A horse weighs twelve hundred pounds;
I weigh only forty.
The turpentine-slug exploded
and I inhaled it,
all of it,
straight into my lungs
and began coughing.
My eyes and ears were on fire
My throat and heart, my very *essence*
was in flames.
Turpentine vapors shot from my nostrils
as if from a dragon's;
To light a match in that room would have been disastrous.

I fell over on my side and went
immediately into convulsions.
He scooped me up in his arms
shouted my name
shouted "HOMER!"
I could hear him shouting
calling me
like he was a long, long way away
and though I was shaking, convulsing
as if electrocuted
I roused myself from that near-place,
the one where he was calling me away from
and, as ever, I came to his call.

We rushed ninety miles an hour,
forty miles to town, to the
emergency room,
with which I was much familiar.
We left Ann sunning herself
on the porch: basking.

I shook and rattled the whole way
I flooded the truck with the scent of my
turpentine-breath, so that his eyes
were watering; and he was crying, too,
for what he had done to me.
But I made it. I am the Alpha and the Homer.
And I have never, ever, had worms.

We ran and never got tired, all day long.
At night the murmuring calls of chuck-will's-widows
bathed us as we slept.
All of these things are life
All of these things are a gift from him to us,
and from us back to him.
Someone has to be alive to see all this.

He missed the mountains.
His stories were starting to repeat themselves,
filling again and again with the colors green and yellow
while his heart and his body
were longing for the ice colors of blue and white.
It's said that dogs can't see color

but we can feel it, like leaves, like heat,
like cool drafts, and warm scents.

He drove north, he and Elizabeth,
with us, looking for a place with these colors.
We spent the summer roaming the West,
where he had gone to college
before we were born.
Before he knew or dreamed us, and
the way we would change his life—
the way everything, each day, adds up
to change your life, to steer it, turn it.
Dogs know this.
The best thing you can do about this
is to take long naps and let it,
the decay of life,
go on past you, as if uninterested in you—
though it is always interested.
            I can tell by the way he looks at us sometimes
That he wants us to be young again;
That he wants to believe it is all in our minds,
that we have gotten lazy:
that we have not paid close enough attention;
that we have wasted time on too many naps
and that it is all going by so fast, now,
but the truth is we're just getting old. And tired.
Our coats aren't as glossy as they were.
We're lumpier with gristle, now, not muscle.
We snore.

He exercises us daily—
wanting us to become young again.

       But that is not the story, what we are now
That is only one day of the story—
and all the ones that came before today
are more a part of it than today is,
though today will sometime become a part of the story.
       Every dog gets old. That is no story at all.
The one we left by the side of the road
The sister who was hit—she did not get old
But in a way, these days are her days, too.

Skunks; we had found skunks
back in Texas. We caught an armadillo there, too,
followed it down into its hole,
tunneling just behind it, sending up
roostertails of rich brown dirt.
We almost caught it—
just as we almost caught rabbits
and almost caught squirrels.
We have never caught anything,
though it always seemed like we were close,
right on something's tail,
and gaining on it.
It seemed like we were destined for greatness
but we were just hounds, alive.

Right away they knew
it was where they wanted to live
when we drove through the dark woods
and then over the blue mountains
and spied the green valley below
the clear river rushing through it like an arrow,
but pausing too and lingering, in places.
Those two old colors were still there,
green in the meadows, and yellow in the flowers
daisies and lilies and even sunflowers—
but up above were the blue mountains,
blue forests, blue grouse, and the icy spines of glaciers.

He finagled a job caretaking an abandoned hunting lodge
where there were the stuffed violent heads of dozens of
horned beasts, which made our hackles rise,
even though we knew they were dead.
We drove back to Mississippi for the last time. It was late
        summer.
The lodge where we'd be living now
was huge, like a castle. It would be cold in winter.
We said good-bye to friends in Mississippi:
our home, our old home.

He rented a big yellow truck
loaded it all one Saturday
and left that same night.
We slept on the big seat next to him.
The truck rumbled,
it made a vibration that went all the way into us,
it was a powerful truck
taking us into yet another life.

And this is where our years have passed, now—in Montana.
Our third, fourth, fifth,
sixth, seventh, eighth, and now
ninth years: this is where we have spent them.
You can only spend them in one place
and they don't come back.
Sometimes we spend them napping
and other days running to the tops of mountains.
We had to learn about porcupines.
We had to learn about mountain lions and bears.
We had to learn about coyotes.
          The coyotes won't bother you eleven months
out of the year, not if Ann and I
stick together, but when their pups
are young in May and June, look out:
if you get too near their den while their pups are little
they will come after you even if days later, for revenge.

They got me bad, last year; four of them caught me behind
the cabin and opened me from behind to chin:
They had me down and were at my belly.
Ann barreled into them
gave it her all:
ready to die with and for me.
She was ferocious, and chased them off.
I crawled home,
my intestines dragging in the dust.

      I lay on the back porch and almost
bled to death, too weak to even whine,
but at least I got home.
Ann whined for me—
Elizabeth heard her and came out.
We went to the vet in Libby,
with whom I am much familiar.
He cleaned me up, sewed me back together.
It took weeks, but I survived.
I am the Alpha and the Homer
I was made to experience this world
It was created for me—
I was meant to move across it.

      Not forever and ever, but for a few years
A few good sweet years; I will not be denied this life.

It used to be a joke, about
not dying in winter, because
that was when the ground was frozen too hard.
Now it's not a joke.
We still have some more years left
and they will not be the best ones,
but I like a good nap anyway.

     This was the first year, the first winter,
that we have seen that look cross his face,
the realization that if we went now,
it would be almost impossible to dig our grave.
It had always been such a big joke.
I truly don't think he understood
that dogs get old.

They have a daughter now. She loves us
as he and Elizabeth once loved us,
and as we still love them,
as we love all three of them now.
If there is one word a dog has the right to use
it is that one.
People pull their punches, refer to dogs' love
with words such as *loyalty, obedience,* or even *submissiveness,*
but it is love.
     We take long naps in the mountain sun, now,
or try to, while the baby tugs on our ears,
covers us with leaves, grass, and dirt:
trampolines on our ribs, just to hear us grunt.

We all go for walks, each day, the five of us.

        He plants trees. They both do, on special occasions:
birth-trees, birthday trees, anniversary trees—
Maple, apple, cherry, ash and lilacs;
Larch, ponderosa pine, spruce fir and cedar.
As we walk, he talks to Elizabeth about their daughter,
being thirty years old someday and seeing these trees he's
planted for her. He talks about how he'll be
sixty-five, then, and she, thirty, and how she can look at them,
knowing he planted them for her: how big they'll be, then.
He strides from tree to tree, looking up.

We will be thirty years gone, at the time of which
he speaks, casting his thoughts into the future, and sometimes,
as he walks and says these things, he forgets
to look down at us, looks only ahead and beyond.
        When we sleep for good, I would like a tree.
I would like Ann to have a tree, too.
We can be side by side,
on one of the hills that we used to explore.
        My tree will be bigger. I loved him more.
Ann is the one he picked first. But he came back for me.

END

—Homer Bass

Sheila Kohler

Shepherd

Two, naturally, we are two,
It is the most natural thing in the world.
I look down at the ground,
Sniff, follow a scent, enraptured,
Smell the odor of sky, of night rain,
Snarl, growl, hear an unheard sound,
Throw back my head and howl at the haloed moon.
I, naturally, lead you,
You who are blind in the light.

—Rambo

Anne Lamott

Spoon River Sadie Louise

My girl got me two weeks after she saw
Silence of the Lambs. She wanted a guard dog,
but tells people I'm
a little like having
Dinah Shore
come live with you.
But she secretly knows I would kill for her and the boy,
her boy so lovely
that people on the street stop us
when we take him for a walk.
She calls him My roommate, Cindy Crawford.

There is also a cat.
The cat has issues.

There are also two birds the girl got for her fortieth birthday.
The boy named them Haddis and Paddis.
Haddis was the boy.
Haddis passed.
There were no marks on him, but
as I say
the cat has issues.

My girl and our boy wept.

The widow Paddis drowned her sorrow in

birdseed, ostrich-like

after Haddis expired and could not be renewed.

The next day the girl went and bought her a new husband.

The boy named him Felipé. There was a Felipé who played

for the Giants long ago, one of the great Alou brothers.

My girl loves baseball.

The boy loves me.

The boy does not say "L"s yet. He says yunch for lunch

yeaves for leaves

yove for love.

Foweepay for Felipé.

He says my name Sadie Yawise Yamott.

He will be five

soon.

So will I.

I was there when Felipé came to live here.

He and the widow Padis began singing

the second they saw each other.

My girl put him in the cage.

They sang hello,

had featherless sex,

sat together quietly

afterwards

having a smoke.

I was there when my girl's best friend
died last year.
The boy said, She has gone to be with God and God's doctor.
The girl cried forever.

The boy says Drunks drink because they miss Jesus.
My girl used to drink. It shows: for instance. She takes me
almost
everywhere she goes
on foot or in our car.
Sometimes I am there in the backseat and she is
hurrying to get all our errands done before the boy
comes home; like he is the Last Emperor;
and she ends up forgetting me in the car
and only remembers me much much later.
I always pretend not to mind,
because she is my girl, and
there are many moving parts to her life;
and God knows
she is doing the best she can,
but
sometimes I wonder,
Should she really be driving?

She misses her friend.
She lives for the boy.

Sometimes he falls asleep on the floor with me as a pillow
and then the kitty
of all people
falls asleep with us too.
The birds sing. My girl sighs, then thinks to look up, and smiles.

–Sadie Louise

Theology

Kathryn Walker

Flea's Hymn

To the Tune of "All Things Bright and Beautiful"

All things brown and beautiful,
All things brown and small,
All things brown and difficult—
The Big Dog made them all.

—_Flea_

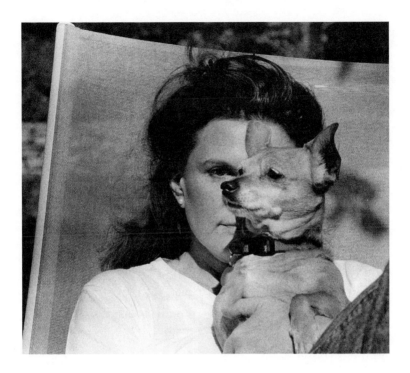

Stephen Dobyns

How to Like It

These are the first days of fall. The wind
at evening smells of roads still to be traveled,
while the sound of leaves blowing across the lawns
is like an unsettled feeling in the blood,
the desire to get in a car and just keep driving.
A man and a dog descend their front steps.
The dog says, Let's go downtown and get crazy drunk.
Let's tip over all the trash cans we can find.
This is how dogs deal with the prospect of change.
But in his sense of the season, the man is struck
by the oppressiveness of his past, how his memories
which were shifting and fluid have grown more solid
until it seems he can see remembered faces
caught up among the dark places in the trees.
The dog says, Let's pick up some girls and just
rip off their clothes. Let's dig holes everywhere.
Above his house, the man notices wisps of cloud
crossing the face of the moon. Like in a movie,
he says to himself, a movie about a person
leaving on a journey. He looks down the street
to the hills outside of town and finds the cut

where the road heads north. He thinks of driving
on that road and the dusty smell of the car
heater, which hasn't been used since last winter.
The dog says, Let's go down to the diner and sniff
people's legs. Let's stuff ourselves on burgers.
In the man's mind, the road is empty and dark.
Pine trees press down to the edge of the shoulder,
where the eyes of animals, fixed in his headlights,
shine like small cautions against the night.
Sometimes a passing truck makes his whole car shake.
The dog says, Let's go to sleep. Let's lie down
by the fire and put our tails over our noses.
But the man wants to drive all night, crossing
one state line after another, and never stop
until the sun creeps into his rearview mirror.
Then he'll pull over and rest awhile before
starting again, and at dusk he'll crest a hill
and there, filling a valley, will be the lights
of a city entirely new to him.
But the dog says, Let's just go back inside.
Let's not do anything tonight. So they
walk back up the sidewalk to the front steps.
How is it possible to want so many things
and still want nothing? The man wants to sleep
and wants to hit his head again and again
against a wall. Why is it all so difficult?
But the dog says, Let's go make a sandwich.

Let's make the tallest sandwich anyone's ever seen.
Wife finds him, staring into the refrigerator
as if into the place where the answers are kept—
the ones telling why you get up in the morning
and how it is possible to sleep at night,
answers to what comes next and how to like it.

Heather McHugh

My Shepherd

A name's another thing
in dog-dom. Fido the Uberpooch is dead,
some singing's overcome the underhund.

The underhund's no private
nose or eye. Smells well, sights bound.
He cops his swill from the bar's back door,
scopes kibble out in big denominations;
even his birthday suit
is finest furs; you'll have
no other dog before me, he rebarks; I'll be
boygone. I'll be

downhome, awaiting his arrival.
What I mean by home is
totally upgussied: I've
got fine pink weenies in the microwave
(he loves paw-long hot-men); I've licked
the floorboards spick, the chain-link span.
I've almost utterly forgotten
any other master (man:

the heaviest
of absentees, you do
the gorge-tattoo, the choke-a-throat. To you

we're Fidos or Rovers,
deep in mastery of mind there is

no other kind). Thank Dog our star
is no cartoon— it's Sirius, not Pluto,
and the one I'm waiting for
won't call me by
my human name. He'll lift

a leg to the polestar, he'll
speak bone; he'll bow and
wow me, nose the moistened
meat. He knows the sweetest
senses of the shady. In the end,

because he cannot lie,

he'll switch me back to Bitch,
from Lady.

Amy Gerstler

Max's Lecture on Canine Buddhism

(Opening Remarks)

All adult dogs I have known embrace Buddhism to some degree.
As puppies, we're too frantic in our heathen frolics to
meditate, recognize delusion, polish a tile with our tongues,
contemplate a waterfall, stare down the endless corridor formed
by a hollowed-out marrow bone. The moment we're housebroken,
though, we begin thinking of ourselves as the night sky, which
never loses its essential character, though thunder may growl
at its edges, and lightning split its endless, forgiving darkness.

—Max

John Rybicki

The Dogman

I hoboed off to escape the dogman, slipping onto the grass
floats below Jefferson. The angels would lift their green
skirts and let me slip in under them and drink at their
shins. I was gliding north through my own body, looping
toward the flaming dog packs, growing wilder. Then he would
whack his hand on my bloodstream and I'd swing a look back
over my shoulder to our house and sink into the mud below
some shrub with my fire spit in half. I'd loop back and
smell where the dogman crossed the Avondale bridge, my
sparks still dripping from his hands. Some days we'd slip
inside my body and pour his light on everything, wild red
hair thick on his body. He'd swipe my mouth left to right
and go out through my eyes to everything.

I would roam through canal water and he'd search for me.
He'd run to the dog packs and they would gather round him,
puffing out their chests, slipping them into the dogman's
hands, letting their hearts bottom and suck through to
his fingers. He needed many of them. When he had enough—
two German Shepherds with cat hair teeth, a Border Collie,
two Huskies, an Australian Shepherd—the dogman would flank
them out in a sweeping net toward the river. But I didn't
want to be found, to be scented down. I crashed out through

the grass, a fanged star, and ripped the Border Collie down
and climbed into her body. The whole pack would gather at
the river after that, a fireball of fang and breath of who
let me through. Then we'd fly apart and spit and tumble in
the grass with the dogman passing his eyes among us.

We'd sniff at each other after that, circling the dogman as
he slipped inside each of our bodies, searching with greased
hands, pouring light, breathing into our wildness to get
me to come out. Christ, you should hear the way my heart
pumps in his hands.

—Charlie

Matthew Graham

Greta's Song

I try to be good.
When the old lady next door yells sit
At her dog, I sit too
For awhile. Then I'm in the air
Chasing birds and my tail, I can't help it
I'm a happy dog
And I sing a song of myself.
It takes so little to be happy—
Something they don't understand—
Just kindness, attention
And a nice yard.
I like my yard, its leaves of grass.
I chew sticks and watch the bees
Mess around in the blue flowers.
But once in a while I bury my best stuff—
My hedgehog, my beer cans—
In places I'll remember, much the way one of them
Might pack a suitcase
And bury it beneath a bed, because even though
They say, "Get down, Greta, it's all right,"
Sometimes doors are slammed inside
And someone is crying.
And you never know, you know?

But I'm a happy dog.
I have no arguments . . . I witness and wait.
What can be wrong in there? I mean,
How much time left together
Can they possibly have
In human years?

—Greta

Mark Doty

Beau: Golden Retrievals

Fetch? Balls and sticks engage my attention
seconds at a time. Catch? I don't think so.
Bunny, tumbling leaf, a squirrel who's—oh
joy—actually scared. Sniff the wind, then

I'm off again: muck, pond, ditch, residue
of any thrillingly dead thing. And you?
Either you're sunk in the past, half our walk,
thinking of what you can never bring back,
or else you're off in some fog concerning
—tomorrow, is that what it's called? My work:
to unsnare time's warp (and woof!), retrieving,
my haze-headed friend, you. This shining bark,

a Zen master's bronzy gong, calls you here,
entirely now: bow-wow, bow-wow, bow-wow.

—Beau

Bernard Cooper

Pet Names

Go ahead. Call me Zacko, Hound Thing, Gray Beard.
Rug Thumper, Fur Face, Curlicue, Nose Head.
Goof Bear, Smudge Pot, Fuzz Bucket, Sonny.

His Dogness, Pasha, Doodle, Black Lips.
Wolf Bane, Mister, Creature, Minky.
Barker. Bone Boy, Will O' the Whisker.

Doggy-Come-Lately, Nanook-of-the-Hearth.
Rutter, Pisser, Sniffer-at-Air.
Chaser-of-Tail, He-Who-Licks-Floor.

I go by none of these names. And more.

—Zachary

Memento
Mori

Walter Kirn

Envoy

I left. I'd finished raising you. I walked
down the drive past the red-flagged mailbox
following the bus that came each day
for you and your brother, who'd played rough with me

once. The problem now was your neglect
as I grew older, an object of respect—
wrapped treats at Christmas, a plaque above my rug:
"No trespassing. Property of Jolly Dog."

All unwanted. Such gentle treatment's harsh
on one who used to scramble through the brush
after cruelly far-flung sticks, or swim
roped behind a boat, if you could catch him.

You always could. I never played hard to get
until you began to go easy. Then I left.

       —Jolly Dog

Susan Minot

Devotion

You left. One by one there were less of you
Less bicycles tipping off their stands
Less leftovers I would get of stew
Less and less shouts and then fewer hands
To pull back my ears and smooth at my head
Or strangle my neck till my tongue got dry.
Some of you changed tastes, slept with cats instead.

Once, apart, you whispered you loved me: a lie.
You went, not I, with a suitcase shut.
I loped after each car. Barks at the end
Of our drive. I could only stray so far. What
I was attached to in you would not stretch or bend.
When the last who'd sucked his bottle sleeping on my
       fleecy side
Left, I ambled off to where dogs bereft alone go,
       and died.

—*Jason*

Alicia Muñoz

Hunting Accident

I heard you park by the road.
Your whistles released me, your
tongue reeled me in.
I pissed through the bars,
inhaling wild boar, baby bats, deer,
a dirt-lipped underworld of rabbits.
I could hear everything, even the geese
snapping crickets by the mill,
where you lay your jacket
in the grass, eating from a can,
your heavy hand of fish and leather
blanketing my eyes.

There's blood in my mouth.
I always find it, soft and still
warm between rotten trunks,
or in a cluster of weeds.
But why do you rock me in your arms,
crying like a bird?

—*Caneli*

Gus Speaks

I was the last of my line,
farm-raised, chesty, and bold.
Not one of your skinny show-world
thirty-five pound Dalmatians.
I ran with the horses, my darlings.

Rivers they forded, wet
to the elbow, I swam. Their lot
was my lot, my lope matching
their stride mile for mile.
Their smell became my smell.

Joyous I ate their manure.
Its undigested oats
still sweet, kept me fit.
I slept with one broodmare.
I curled at her flank.

My head on that bay haunch
we lay, a study in snores,
ear flicks, and farts in her stall
until the hour of her foal.
She shunned me most cruelly.

Spring and fall, I erred over
and over. Skunks were my folly.
Then, I was nobody's lover.
I rolled in dung and sand.
My heart burst in the pond.

My body sank and then rose
like a birch log, a blaze
of white against spring green.
Now I lie under the grasses
they crop, my own swift horses

who start up and spook in the rain
without me, the warm summer rain.

—Caesar Augustus

Coach

All trucks were from Hell and deserved my bite,
All children sheep and not to leave the yard.
Before I came, the house was unsafe;
The man whistled and no one heard,
And the huge trucks lumbered.

When the boy walked out, ball in hand,
I coached. He called me that. "Coach,"
He'd say, and I'd bark back, "Now! Now!"
Till the game was "Here Coach, Fetch Coach,"
And I was off and straightway back, unless,
Of course, one of the trucks from Hell passed by.

Thrown objects were my specialty,
The lazy sticks, their high trajectories,
That, and the knack I had for words—
Here, fetch, hunt, stay, sit, lie-down . . .
And names, for the boy, his sister.
I lived those names twelve years, a diplomat
Who read the world four different ways,
Nose, ear, eye, and sometimes what was said.

When my coat thinned, legs stiffened and I
Turned deaf, I was practical; I didn't run,
Limped wisely over, once the stick had plopped.
Then the children left, as sticks were lost,
As the man's whistle rose past hearing,
As all sounds stopped, and I was nose and eye,
Watching the trucks from Hell roll by,
Each silent and deserving of my bite,
Which the last one got, till I never let go.

—Morgan

Edward Albee

Samantha

They weren't with me
When I was taken in to die.
They were in Spain.

They lay on a bed in Grenada
With the phone to their ear
And they cried when they told them,
Cried into the phone.

I know that much.

I was kept for them
Curled in a frozen sleep
Until they came back.

They dug a hole then
(He and his friend dug a hole then)
On the point, by the ocean
Where all the others had been laid:
Poochie, Jennifer, Harry, Andrew, Jane
        and the cats
Cunegonde, Sarah, Leslie, Dorothy, Jake.

They dug a hole and put me in it.
Gentle Diane, the potter,
Baked clay biscuits for me
Placed them.
(Very Egyptian for an Irish Wolfhound

      —but nice.)

I liked being with all the others,
On the point, by the ocean,
Especially Andrew, especially Jake.

I wonder—

    when it comes time
For the diggers, for gentle Diane,
Will they be put here too?
On the point? By the ocean? With us?

I hope so.

Kate Clark Spencer

When I Died on My Birthday

My heart broke for you.
I nudged your face while you called my
name over and over and
cried no until there was no sound.
You couldn't feel it.

Strange seeing your own
body lying on the grass. My
eyes were slits, my ears
black triangles. And my long legs
were tan and smooth as

polished oak. Not moving. You were
desperate, so I
gave you butterflies, the symbol
of the soul and of
rebirth. I prompted Kim to buy

a book of butterflies, gemlike,
the microscopic
photographs, you said, dazzled you.
I got Max to grab
that tablecloth her mother made

embroidered in thread
with seven butterflies. Andy
made a cloth and wood
dog you used to show me. Yes, I
knew the dog was me.

Butterflies weaved into the silk
were rust-brown like me,
and iridescent. I was in
the canyon when a
butterfly followed

you along the creek where you found
my stone. And I watched
you press your cheek against the words
you had Kris sandblast:
BELL we will discuss butterflies.

—Bell

Anderson Ferrell

Out

Casey
b. May 10, 1981
d. July 14, 1994

From two voices I learned some words
and loved three.
Out—a place I ran ahead to.
Dirk—who I shared with one not Dirk.
Chevy—what I rode in to places where I forgot
words and remembered my blood.

But I am to go now. That is my will, but my will
they taught me,
mostly.
Dirk and the one not Dirk.

The one not Dirk says the word
we both love the most.
Then he says *Chevy*.
My blood reminds itself.
The needle pricks.
He says *Out*,
and I wag my tail and go there;
knowing and running—
without a look back,
that they, though lagging,
not smelling what tugs at my nose,
not hearing who else calls me,
have no will but to follow.

—*Casey*

Gerald Stern

The Dog

What I was doing with my white teeth exposed
like that on the side of the road I don't know,
and I don't know why I lay beside the sewer
so that lover of dead things could come back
with his pencil sharpened and his piece of white paper.
I was there for a good two hours whistling
dirges, shrieking a little, terrifying
hearts with my whimpering cries before I died
by pulling the one leg up and stiffening.
There is a look we have with the hair of the chin
curled in mid-air, there is a look with the belly
stopped in the midst of its greed. The lover of dead things
stoops to feel me, his hand is shaking. I know
his mouth is open and his glasses are slipping.
I think his pencil must be jerking and the terror
of smell—and sight—is overtaking him;
I know he has that terrified faraway look
that death brings—he is contemplating. I want him
to touch my forehead once and rub my muzzle
before he lifts me up and throws me into
that little valley. I hope he doesn't use
his shoe for fear of touching me; I know,

or used to know, the grasses down there; I think
I knew a hundred smells. I hope the dog's way
doesn't overtake him, one quick push,
barely that, and the mind freed, something else,
some other thing, to take its place. Great heart,
great human heart, keep loving me as you lift me,
give me your tears, great loving stranger, remember
the death of dogs, forgive the yapping, forgive
the shitting, let there be pity, give me your pity.
How could there be enough? I have given
my life for this, emotion has ruined me, oh lover,
I have exchanged my wildness—little tricks
with the mouth and feet, with the tail, my tongue is a parrot's,
I am a rampant horse, I am a lion,
I wait for the cookie, I snap my teeth—
as you have taught me, oh distant and brilliant and lonely.

Stephen Dunn

Buster's Visitation

I'm a dead dog for real now;
no longer can I rise
from my fakery, alert to commands
I'd come to think of as love,
though I never did obey
as well as Sundown did
or as a truly good dog would.
To play the slave, not be one,
was my code. You understood,
who would play the master.
From my grave in the yard I see now
you had no gift for it, or heart.
Bad dog, you'd say,
so little conviction in your voice.
In seconds you'd be patting my head.
Forgiveness made you happy; I'd tip over
the garbage to be forgiven by you.
Let me tell you it's no life
being dead. I'd give anything
to chase the gulls again.
But clarities come when the body goes.
For whatever it's worth

you should know—you who think so much—
only what's been smelled or felt
gets remembered.
And in the dark earth no doors open,
no one ever comes home.

—Buster

Ben Sonnenberg

Harry
_1981-1992_
d. March 13

Stay

I was a bad dog and didn't obey
Any command, until today.

> —_Harry_

Page xi:	Mace the Dog Boy	67:	Kenneth Chen
18:	Arnold Mesches	69:	Robert Benson
19:	Kenneth Chen	70:	Kate Bernhardt
20:	Kenneth Chen	77:	Bob Frishman
23:	Kenneth Chen	83:	Kenneth Chen
24:	Josefa Mulaire	86:	Brother Paul Diveny
25:	Kenneth Chen	98:	Miriam Berkley
26:	Merrill Markoe	101:	Vince Leo
29:	Martha Baxter	105:	Kenneth Chen
30:	Kenneth Chen	107:	Inge Morath
33:	Connie McGovern	111:	Elizabeth Hughes Bass
35:	Lucinda Johnson	113:	Elizabeth Hughes Bass
39:	Sidney Wade	117:	Elizabeth Hughes Bass
41:	Kenneth Chen	121:	Elizabeth Hughes Bass
44:	Joan Ackerman	132:	Kenneth Chen
48:	Palos Verdes Police Department	136:	Brian Conway
		139:	Kathryn Walker
50:	Kenneth Chen	145:	Benjamin Weissman
53:	Geoff Winningham	151:	Kenneth Chen
54:	E. J. Camp	154:	Millie Kirn
57:	Merrill Markoe	159:	Judith Moyer
58:	Miriam Berkley	167:	Don Steffy
63:	Steve Bull	169:	Peter Feldstein
65:	Kenneth Chen	173:	Susanna Sonnenberg